THOMAS A. DORSEY FATHER OF BLACK GOSPEL MUSIC

AN INTERVIEW

Genesis of Black Gospel Music

∽

ROBERT L. TAYLOR

Order this book online at www.trafford.com
or email orders@trafford.com

Most Trafford titles are also available at major online book retailers.

Printed in the United States of America.

ISBN: 978-1-4907-2235-1 (sc)
ISBN: 978-1-4907-2236-8 (e)

Trafford rev. 12/19/2013

 www.trafford.com

North America & international
toll-free: 1 888 232 4444 (USA & Canada)
fax: 812 355 4082

Preface

Thomas A. Dorsey—not to be confused with the white band leader of the same name—was born in Villa Rica, Georgia, in 1899. The eldest son of an itinerate Baptist preacher, Mr. Dorsey enthusiastically spoke to the writer of this paper of his travels with his father. "We went to many places. I got to know a little more about that life than the average person . . . that's when I first began to get to know people—what I mean is know the inside of people, musically and all other ways."

When Dorsey moved from Atlanta to Chicago, he picked up the name of "Georgia Tom."

"Georgia Tom had blues in his mind as well as in his hands and feet," says Arna Bontemps.[1] "He had composed Ma Rainey's popular theme music 'Rain on the ocean / Rain on the deep blue sea' as well as scores of other blues. If the blues idiom meant anything to you, he was your boy."[2]

Within two years, "Georgia Tom was able to turn a Saturday night stomp upside down with his playing." In those days, however, Dorsey had more on his mind than playing piano. For one thing, there was a girl.[3] "When she looked at Tom he felt like a boy dazzled by the sun. Then, quite suddenly, her family moved to Birmingham, carrying

---

[1] Patterson, *Rock, Church, Rock,* 77.

[2] Ibid.

[3] Ibid., 78.

the daughter with them." It broke Tom's heart.[4] "In his mood . . . ambition was born."[5]

First he tried, with such local help as he could get, to teach himself harmony, composition, instrumentation, and arranging. "He went to work at the steel mills of Gary, Indiana, which made the wages of a Georgia Stomp musician look sick. The steel mill all but did his thin 128-pound body in, but he kept at it until he could get a five-piece orchestra together."[6]

This orchestra marked the beginning of Georgia Tom. It gave him piano practice and it enabled him to earn money by playing for parties in the steel mill communities of Gary and South Chicago. It provided exercise in the making of band arrangements and piano scores, and it left time for study at the Chicago College of Composition and Arranging.

Dorsey joined the Pilgrim Baptist Church in 1921, which, as it turned out, was the year the National Baptist Convention met in Chicago. A song called "I Do, Don't You," C. A. Tindley its composer, caused people attending the convention to be lifted from their chairs. The song started a wheel turning in the heart of Dorsey and lifted young Dorsey as nothing he had pounded out at parties or stomps. To Bontemps, gospel music was his calling. But Dorsey continued to write the blues.

One of the early blues songs that Georgia Tom composed was entitled "Count the Days I'm Gone." "The wastebasket got that," said Arna Bontemps. A few years later, together with Tampa Red, Georgia Tom commenced a series of blues under the name "Georgia

---

[4] Ibid.

[5] Ibid.

[6] Ibid.

Tom." One, "It's Tight like That," became a smash hit. Song followed song, and when Dorsey got sick and was unable to work for eighteen months, his newly acquired wife had to go to work in a laundry shop.[7] It was just what he needed; he commenced to improve immediately.[8]

It occurred to Dorsey that perhaps his sickness was less of the body and more of the mind. To prove it, he sat down and wrote a new song—one of his ringing successes, "Someday, Somewhere." The song was widely approved by church people of all denominations throughout the Christian world, but no publisher wanted it. Dorsey, at his own expense, had one thousand copies printed. Nobody would buy them. The choirs or musical directors were impressed. The only thing left to Dorsey was to get out and sing his song to the people themselves.[9]

Eventually, the Brunswick Recording Company rescued him by giving him a job arranging music for their recording artists.

Later on, Dorsey toured the country (USA) with Sallie Martin, another Georgia native who lived in Chicago. Dorsey would play, Ms. Martin would sing. Money was scarce; sales were slow. The songs were finally heard, and in 1932, he and Ms. Martin founded the National Convention of Gospel Choirs and Choruses, granting the nascent art form an institutional status. (In 1972, the organization convened in Washington, DC, attracting twelve thousand delegates.)

From the beginning, gospel songs found favor with white evangelists and publishers whose church audiences shared the poverty

---

[7.] Ibid., 79.

[8.] Ibid.

[9.] Ibid.

and religious fundamentalism of Dorsey's flock. By the late thirties, his songs were included in major white hymnals published in the Deep South. Dorsey's success continued though his earnings never touched those of comparable writers in other genres.

Introduction

Mr. Thomas Andrew Dorsey's telephone number was given to the writer of this paper by a directory assistance operator in Chicago, Illinois. The writer took a chance and called, not expecting the first publisher[10] of black gospel music to answer the phone. A very hoarse voice said "Hello," and the writer recognized it immediately as being the voice he had heard on a recording about gospel music that Mr. Dorsey had done. After being asked if he would consent to being interviewed, Mr. Dorsey unenthusiastically said yes. He was unenthusiastic, the writer later discovered, because fortune hunters and status seekers had been plaguing him for interviews. Honored that Mr. Dorsey had said yes, the writer took a train from Kansas City, Missouri, to Chicago to see this man who had written hundreds of songs.

A mansion, servants, and a limousine is what the writer expected as a part of Mr. Dorsey's life, but he had quite a modest home, a very cordial wife, and an earlier-model car. Mr. Dorsey was to be found in the rear of the house, in a small room decorated with numerous plaques and trophies. He was lying down, wrapped in bandages, in the process of recuperating from an automobile accident.

The accident, he said, had not been too serious, and he made it clear that "Providence" had probably arranged our interview because he had forgotten our appointment. This thin white-haired elderly

---

10. Tallmadge, *Responsorial and Antiphonal Practice in Gospel Songs*, 219.

gentleman was full of energy at times and, at other times, very, very quiet. Although Mr. Dorsey explained that he did not have much formal education, the writer was in awe at the words and wit of this unsung hero in American history. The writer would like to thank Mr. Dorsey for the hours we shared.

The Interview

TAYLOR. Were you born in Chicago?

DORSEY. No, I was born in Atlanta, Georgia, about twenty-five miles out of Atlanta.

TAYLOR, *kidding*. Do you remember what year?

DORSEY. Sure, I gotta remember that or I won't get my social security. In 1899.

TAYLOR. So you spent time in Atlanta?

DORSEY. Well, let's go at it like this. My father was an itinerate preacher, Baptist preacher. We traveled from place to place. Didn't get too far at a time, but I went with him. I was the eldest son, and we went to many places. I got to know a little more about life than the average person, than a boy who didn't go, just stayed home. That's where I first started to begin to know people, what I mean is to know the inside of people and musically and all other ways. My mother was a musician and played the organ at church. I remember that to be about 1903 or 1904.

TAYLOR. How long have you been in Chicago?

DORSEY. I've been here since 1916. I've seen world wars going on. I came packaging war goods and one thing or another. Just about drafted me before the war started.

TAYLOR. What was some of your early training?

DORSEY. Now you could take when I was a boy. You'd have to be fifty-five years or older. Music was a very important thing in the church and theater. Movie houses didn't have much. Canned music was in the movie houses—music that played itself.

TAYLOR. Player piano music?

DORSEY. Yeah—Vaudeville music where acts came in was another place you could find music. In Atlanta where I grew up, I sold pop in the theater. That's where Eddie Hayward and his father played. And I got a chance too, selling pop there, to learn music. As you know, my father was an itinerate preacher, going from place to place, and I'd stick around until good-time night (Saturday night). Fellows would come in from the country and have a good time with the gals. They needed somebody to play an old-time piano. Only thing you had to watch they got raided. One night, I recall I was going into a place and I couldn't figure my way out. I always figure my way out just in case I might have to leave unannounced. I figure my way out even if I were go to your house. I always have that at the tip of my fingertips and so I went over there. It was hot weather. The exit was down between two buildings. A big guy couldn't get down there. Believe it or not, I had to go out that window. I went across the street.

TAYLOR. What were the people doing?

DORSEY. Oh, nothing. Just dancing, having a little fun, but you see the law was bad. They didn't want any black folk to have pleasure at all. Just raid the place and make them stay in jail over the weekend if not longer. I tried to play for those fellows. Of course, those were the only places you could play. I played all over town when there was something going on with people like Lockleed Nonbush, a fellow called

Longboy, and James A. Ray, names that won't mean very much to you and Eddie Hayward. His son wrote "Canadian Sunset," so those are the kind of things you had to come in contact with to get anywhere. You didn't make money half the time, but you got all the liquor you could drink if you drank. So out of all that, what I'm trying to say now or work up to is out of all that, I got the greatest training and experience of my life.

Everybody can't, every musician can't sit down and talk about life, even that kind of life. The type of music—black music—they played back there wasn't published, and if it hadn't been for Handy, you would not have any, any blues published. Handy was interested enough in it to soak money into it. He used to have a place here in Chicago down State Street here. Yet it's wonderful to see how a little thing can grow. It seems to be a little thing, but when you begin to delve into it and turn it outside in, it turns out to be a big thing. Sometimes bigger than in someways you can handle.

TAYLOR. Did you do anything aside from music?

DORSEY. Play baseball. But a—no—music was not a hobby with me, it was a business. No, I've always found something to do in music. In Atlanta, as I said, I played all over town. Black fellows didn't have the money to pay you. As I said, they'd give you all the liquor you could drink. If it wasn't a drinkin' party, you had to slip your bottle in to spike the punch when nobody was lookin'. But it was enjoyable to me as well as educational. The type of music that I [was] trying to become interested in, of course I couldn't play at home until my folks had gone away. My mother had an organ, and she'd go away and I'd ring those blues on that organ.

TAYLOR. Did you ever compose for any other media other than vocal or choral such as for the piano or other instruments?

DORSEY. I may have some instrumental. I wasn't for that. That's too long and drawn out. First place, it had to sell. You've got to sell it to an instrumentalist. You get some guy who could belt out a song. If they heard it first-time people would buy that way ten times as fast as they would instrumental. Instrumental music did not appeal to me, not for a business like that.

TAYLOR. Did you play solo any instruments like the piano or organ?

DORSEY. Yes. I played piano, I played organ, played guitar, used to play some of everything except wind instruments. Wind instruments were too hard for me. I used to play violin too, back in the show days.

TAYLOR. What were some of the highlights of your blues career?

DORSEY. Well, I was an orchestra and band leader. I worked with the big people like Ma Rainey and Bessie Smith. In that, we got the chance to meet nearly everybody in the Theater Owner's Booking Association circuit. That's what they called Theaters, Buckers, Owners Association or something like that. You were lucky if you got your money most of the time. That's the only circuit we got to play. There were some of the big fellows—Shelton Brooks that played the Orphan Circuit. The white circuit took others way out to the coast. But till I got along all right on the circuit, it fit right for me. You see the blues singers fit right in there. Ma Riney was one of the greatest blues singers. In fact, I knew her here in Chicago. I used to play for her recordings before I took the band with her. I think that's one of the most striking incidents in my life. When I got a chance to work with Ma, Al Wynn, Gable Washington—dead now had about a seven-piece band. They traveled too. Some other perfomers got laid off. Ma's was a power. We got where we wanted. We got any town, any hotel, but of course in those days, you couldn't get into white hotels. We got the best colored hotels though. Some white folks made it convenient for you though. We even stayed in white folks' houses.

TAYLOR. Were there any significant gospel music highlights?

DORSEY. No, gospel music hadn't come into being then. It was being made in me then. Howls and sad moans they had in blues, I brought over and put it in gospel music and made them work. That's the reason gospel singers got over. They got something there that touches the people that you just don't touch otherwise. And it's one of those things. I don't know what to call it, but I can take to any congregation right now. I'm not much of a singer, but I can take the blues and do the same thing. Now that's two things that really belong to black men and black women. They will nurture the thing.

TAYLOR. So what you're saying then is that gospel music was birthed out of the blues.

DORSEY. Now I don't say it exactly like that. Now it is a very important relative. Something like that, for lack of a better term, for after all, gospel is good news. Blues, ain't she a good woman feelin' bad? She just lookin' for good news. Of course, you can fix it up like you want it. It all dovetails right in there together. But now they're trying to change things around so much I don't bother with them. I let them change it. I've got mine out of it. (*Laughs.*)

TAYLOR, *laughs*. I have this gospel music thing on the inside. I'm interested in trying to make America realize that gospel music is as important as the spiritual or more so.

DORSEY. The gospel is more important than the spiritual. The spiritual was just a spontaneous outburst. It was many, many years before the spiritual was on paper. We had to be, some of us had to be cultivated to put it on the paper.

TAYLOR. You say the spiritual was a spontaneous outburst?

DORSEY. Sure, that's all it is. Folks felt the way they sang. You know they were out there, in there, in the cotton fields where they were singing. Nobody had written the stuff down. If they had written it down, who was going read it?

TAYLOR. Why do you feel that gospel music is more impotant than the spiritual?

DORSEY. Because it's good news to the world and it has spoken for itself. I don't have to speak for it. I'm just an instrument. Gospel—I'll tell you how I came here to Chicago in the thirties when Hitler was raising so much sand. I was on a train in the Indiana hills—I don't say mountains when they're that long. We went through a big thing like a pasture. There were sheep, goats, cows, horses, and mules all out there grazing on the hill. I could see men rolling down the hillside. I said why in the devil do those fools in Europe try to have wars there as peaceful as this valley is. "Peace in the Valley," one of the greatest numbers I ever wrote was right there. I picked the song out of the war. So you can't ever tell if you got something. Don't throw it away or let it get away from you. "Don't go to sleep on the job," most men say. Don't go to sleep no time and nowhere 'cause you can't tell where your startin' point may create. Let me tell you about this.

My first wife, Nettie—she's the one that died in 1932—here while I was away. I have a son and a daughter now as well as my second wife. My daughter has two children and my son has two children. But let me tell you about this. I had gotten into the gospel business then and published a few things. I was down in St. Louis advertising my stuff. They sent me a telegram saying my wife had just died. She was having a baby and I said that can't be so. I called on the phone—it was so. So one young man, happens he was a singer and he drove down with me, he said, "I'm gonna drive you back to Chicago tonight." We drove on back and so. They never moved the body. I had a lovely bouncing baby there—nice looking fellow, by golly. He looked better than I did, and I said maybe this one ain't mine. I was trying to keep myself together—but that night the baby died. Ain't that something? I didn't know how to handle something like that, but I put my wife away, baby in the casket. I had just gotten a job directing a choir.

TAYLOR. What church?

DORSEY. Pilgrim Baptist Church in Indiana. After putting her away, I didn't throw away my old blues records. Most of the blues had become stale and wasn't selling so the gospel idea began to kinda grow on me a little. And then everything I wrote was gospel, gospel, gospel, gospel. That's the way gospel songs got started. They didn't call them that. You couldn't go into my church where I am now, and I've been there forty years or no other church talkin' about gospel songs. Man, they'd throw you out of there "You can't sing no gospel, you got to preach the gospel. You're getting into the preacher's way now."

Taylor. What were the church people singing then?

Dorsey. They were singing hymns out of the brown book. You didn't call them gospel. I took the word up and put it to gospel songs and said gospel song. Man, this thing caught fire, went all over the country, and has been all over the world now. I didn't do the whole job alone. God was my help. Now as I told you about the gospel song, you'd better not go gettin' in preacher's way.

Taylor. Getting in the preacher's way?

Dorsey. Yeah, you preachin' on his territory. I coined the word, and I kept hammerin' away, beatin' it around here in Chicago. And a few singers were I guess willin' to risk their lives. Sallie Martin was one of them. She and I met the great lady, Ms. Dennis. She was a trained singer. She tried to do too many things. What I'm trying to say is she didn't stick to one thing. I met Ms. Martin out there one night, and Ms. Dennis was teachin' her. She had Ms. Martin there tryin' to make a note high as a house and she was a contralto.

Taylor, *laughs.*

Dorsey. There was no hope. All I was a little old bandleader. I brought the note down to her where [she] could get it. Both of them admitted it sounded better. That's where I met Ms. Martin. I tried to get rid of Ms. Martin, but I never could get rid of Ms. Martin, so I hired her in my place. She worked for me until she went out for herself.

Taylor. Who were some of the famous people whose lives you may have influenced? I read in different articles that people like Mahalia Jackson and James Cleveland made contact with you.

Dorsey. Well, we had something to do with each other. First place, I don't care how good you are or how talented you were if you have any place to display it, it was nil. I had a place to display it see.

Taylor. Where was that?

Dorsey. All over the country. I told you that I was in show business for a long time. I had some places to go.

Taylor. Did any of them go with you?

Dorsey. Yeah. Mahalia traveled with me three or four years. I put her on the map. And Clara Ward was one of my protégés. I used to stop at her mother's house so many years ago. Time has taken it away from me.

Taylor. What about James Cleveland?

Dorsey. Oh, yeah. When he was a boy, he was around pickin' up the crumbs, gettin' them together.

Taylor. The crumbs? What do you mean by the crumbs?

Dorsey. Well, gettin' all the information you can stand around and get. James didn't have no direct connection. Of course, he's got a direct connection now and has had it for years. But there was a time when we didn't any of us have no connection. What I mean was that there was nobody to even publish or sing your stuff. Sallie didn't have it. I didn't have it. When James was a boy, I used to put him in my choir. I let him come on Sunday morning to play and direct—maybe give him a dollar fifty cents. Well, that was encouragement. I mean he was a boy. Any of them that's anything, I touched somewhere or they touched me. You see the thing about it is that I didn't go after it to try to get rich—one of them kind of things. Shoot, I just want to live. Many singers got off the scene without being known. Like I was speaking about Ms. Ward, Clara Ward's mother is a great singer. Clara was the one who died. I think her mother's still living.

TAYLOR. Yes. Clara Ward's mother is still living and Clara died.

DORSEY. Many cold nights, I'd come in. Can you put me up? Yeah, come on in.

TAYLOR. Who would say that, Clara?

DORSEY. Clara Ward's mother, who was a singer also. Clara was a singer since she was that high. (*Pointing a couple of feet from the floor.*) She was quite a prodigy. So many others. I remember once they [had] a big thing downtown here [Chicago]. Soldier's Field. They used "My Precious Lord" on it. Didn't nobody know what "Precious Lord" was then. Boy, that thing raised those people out of their seats. Now nobody got any business hollering *amen* at a musical festival. That's what they were doing. That was years and years ago. A. J. Wesley Jones and James A. Monday. Jones was directing. Now get those names and put them in a book. Now they're somebody you should write about.

TAYLOR. Who were those two men?

DORSEY. Two of the greatest religious music directors, arrangers, and composers in the country.

TAYLOR. Out of Chicago? Still living?

DORSEY. Yeah. Monday's still living, but Wesley's dead. Boatner used to direct at my church. Monday's one of the country's greatest black musicians. But the black musicians don't know him. He's too old—I guess to bother with him. But that's where you're going to find that stuff. You've got to go back and get it from the fellows who had it way back there.

TAYLOR. I like the arrangement that Aretha Franklin has recorded of your "Precious Lord" with the addition of Carol King's "You've Got a Friend." Do you know Aretha personally?

DORSEY. Do I know her? I used to know her when she was like that. (*Pointing two feet from the floor.*) Her dad used to come to my church. He used to run revivals, and I used to go and sing in Detroit when they lived in Detroit years ago. This thing just didn't start.

TAYLOR. Are you familiar with Edwin Hawkins and Andraé Crouch?

DORSEY. Yes. All of them can't be alike. That's the reason I'm what I am. Wasn't no need of me trying to do what someone else was doin'. I happened on the scene at the point when the people wanted somethin' new—wanted somethin' with life.

TAYLOR. Are your works collected in one place, and if so, does the collector have a list of your complete works?

DORSEY. Yes, sir. Guarded and stored away. I publish a lot of different types of music under different labels. It's out there. If you get anything the folks want, take it out there. They'll take it. If they don't take it, they don't want it. They publish my stuff under different labels—even under all kinds of foreign languages. Of course, I can't read them. Ain't no need of keepin' them around here. Hill and Range Publishing Company, my publisher. I happened to be one of the lucky ones who got in on the ground floor about twenty-three or twenty-four years ago.

TAYLOR. Have you ever been to Europe?

DORSEY. Oh yeah, several times. My wife and I just came back a year ago. I've been to France, Italy, and even Jerusalem. One of my biggest outlets in Europe is in Italy. My publisher,

Hill and Range, is there. I was their guest man. They wined and dined my wife and I quite a bit.

Taylor. What organization or group sponsored you there?

Dorsey. My publisher, Hill and Range. Even in Rome, I used to write blues. Some were popular like "Storm Sea Blues." There was a place in Rome—a nightclub called Big Top. Being a songwriter or musician you were chauffeured. My wife and I had a big to-do down there. The nightclub had a gospel songwriter, Dorsey. Tommy Dorsey, not—not Tommy Dorsey. I'll tell you a little joke later. The joke is true. I got in there with the man—and was a star around there.

Taylor. Were you singing and playing?

Dorsey. Yes. I sang and played popular songs, anything. Sure I could do the same thing now if I wanted to. I had a big time—a big time. So that was one of the things I did from there on that Big Top place. That was my company. I didn't have to tell them I was goin' to Rome. I didn't have to find a place because they saw to it that I had a hotel. Now that was wonderful and all because I was a gospel songwriter. Of course, I went back and got the old blues and asked the people do you remember the old blues? Some of those things still sell now and I get paid.

In one of our travels, we were in Jerusalem. My company, Hill and Range, has publishing houses all over the world. I told them I think I'm goin' to Jerusalem. My wife and I had heard there was a Baptist Church. I knew I had given permission some years ago for them to put "Precious Lord" in Yiddish or Jewish, and I wanted to go to this Baptist Church and see what happened. We went there one bright Sunday morning. Got to the door, gave them one of my cards. "Ya Mr. Thomas Dorsey?" I said yeah. Sent the card down to the minister man or whatever. The man said come on down here. This is supposed to be a Jewish Baptist Church. They got them all over the world.

Taylor. Jewish Baptist?

Dorsey. Yeah man, that's the reason you have to travel around and see what's goin' on. "Now we got Thomas Dorsey, the man who wrote 'Precious Lord Take My Hand.' Come on down, brother Dorsey, and lead us in the song." Handed me a hymnbook written in Hebrew.

Taylor, *laughs*.

Dorsey. Good thing I knew my song. "Well, I'm from America and I have to do English and I want you to go with me." I'm tellin' the Lord *don't leave me now, don't leave me now*. Man, we got to singin', and those Jews went wild. Not only there, yeah even on the north side of Chicago. Sallie can tell you about it.

We were traveling on the road to Damascus and stopped at one of the oases. I went back to the washroom. I met a white fellow back there. He said, "My name is Jones." I said, "My name is Dorsey, the man who writes songs." I said to one of them. I knew Tommy—he's dead—he died last year. No, I'm talkin' about the man who writes gospel songs. I turned it off politely. Shoot, that guy had gone outside. When I got outside, he told everybody "there's the man who wrote 'Precious Lord Take My Hand.'" When I got out there, the folks were saying "sing, sing, sing, sing." Heck, I can't even sing at home, let alone when its ninety degrees in the shade. I sang the verse, and they sang the chorus. Shoot, everybody got to singin' that song. Arabs—everybody.

Taylor. So do you feel that gospel music can be a learned thing or does it have to be inspired by God?

Dorsey. Well—both. But the last one first—inspired by God.

Taylor. Well, how do you teach it to white people, Jewish, or Arabs? If they want to teach it to somebody, how do you get it over to them to teach?

Dorsey. Well, now that's the ninety-nine dollar question. That's the question. There's something that goes along with it. How you don't preach it and you don't teach it. I don't teach it—ain't no man can teach it. But there's something in gospel music. You know there must be something, else it wouldn't have the coverage it's made throughout the world. Whatever that is, that's what you got to enlarge on. Some say it's the Spirit. Some say it's a shout. Some say this, that, and the other. Now don't ask me. I don't know what it is—only thing is it got me over, and I'm not going to change mine. I'm satisfied with it.

Taylor. Get one thing and keep it?

Dorsey. Keep it. As to the question, maybe you'll find out by and by. I can't answer that question. So whatever it is, I'd like to know myself.

Taylor. Do you feel it is important that gospel musicians educate themselves and get training at the university level?

Dorsey. Yes, sir, you want to know more than one thing. Your musicians should know something about all of it. I even studied, but it was all Greek to me. But I studied and could talk on it. I needed it. There did come a time when I got a chance to talk to people who knew about it and were in it and who helped me. My publishers in New York (Hill and Range) didn't just want to publish gospel songs or popular songs—they wanted to cover the whole field.

There was a wonderful act of luck—or a blessing. A man came here to my home a few years ago, sat down an hour until he got through talking. I said well, I was very busy. You see, I was trying to get rid of him. He said, "Well, it may interest you to know that a publishing house in New York sent me out here to see you and several others. It might interest you to know also that I have an advanced check for $200 in this pocket." So we started over again, sat right there, signed all the contracts. They sent my kids to college and everything. I don't have to bother about my music in Europe, Asia, or wherever my music is. They collect for me. So never can tell what's coming your way, and I think the black man made his mistake. He wasn't aware of these things. There was not enough awareness, and there was not enough profundity. The black man did not have it deep enough in his system. So in this business, I got plaques and stuff. I don'know where they all are. I've been places where I thought I would never get to go. People have been here from all over the world and have talked with me about gospel music. And not for anything that I have done and not from anything that I know so much. I'm not a great authority on it, but I'm the best authority right down through here. Now these youngsters coming up, they get hungry fast. They try to switch and change it around to get the quick buck. After a while, they'll find out that the quick buck will be gone. They have no foundation to stand on. So it's been interesting to me. I was a blues singer turned around, and I made money at it. But now a fellow like you comes along. Man, now you go to some of those big guys even now—I'm not talkin' about gospel. Some of these guys that run these big shows now couldn't sit down and talk to him like you're talking to me—don't care how much money you had—Just too important, too rich, too this, that, and the other. Now I'm not saying this because I need some money 'cause I ain't got any now, but I know where to get it. My publisher never lets me down.

Another thing, if these Negroes gonna get in the world with whatever production, go up there callin' it a black production, a white production, or a yellow production. Go produce what you have and put it to the man, let him decide what it's to be called, then it's all right. Now don't do away with the word *black*, but let the thing work itself out before you give it it's label. See what I mean. You don't know whether you want the thing or not. Go on and do your thing, then at the right psychological moment, unfold your label. I'm not against black, I'm not against white—I'm not against anything produced in the United States. European money, any kind like that I'm with. I helped with the Black Movement—didn't get nothing. Shoot, I know some guys who did—if they did, why couldn't I get mine. Everythings gonna come out fine. What I'm trying to say is the information you're getting from me, you're not going to get from anybody else. I ain't got time to fool for them that pay for it. That's where Sallie Martin got all of her information. She came down, and I gave her a job at the studio. Been all over the country. She didn't have no money. I didn't either. I had some songs—if we could sell some songs, we could make it from town to town.

Taylor. Do you remember Gwendolyn Dixon? She lives in Kansas City, Missouri, and is about the only person who sells gospel sheet music there.

Dorsey. I don't know.

Taylor. I asked because she told me she met you at St. Stephen's Church in Kansas City.

Dorsey. It's been a long time since I've been to Kansas City. Wherever they sold gospel music, I was there some time or another.

Taylor. I see "Doctor Thomas Dorsey" on some of the plaques you have on display.

Dorsey. "Doctor Thomas A. Dorsey" doesn't mean any doctor so many places. I don't even know where they come from. I got one from a school in Ohio. I take and bury them. Believe it or not, they honor those too. I'm not going to do anything to take from the honor. If you want me to be a doctor, I'll be a doctor. It's strange, but after all when you put together, it means so much. Not all this junk. (*Referring to the room full of plaques and trophies.*) It ain't because I did so much. The source must have come from some other. I didn't do any more than just sing the songs, and wherever I go, it has helped so many others. So many other would-be gospel songwriters wanted to write the songs or wanted to do this or that, so I say it's just a great blessing to me, that's all. Not for anything that I've done, I've just jumped from one thing to another. But whatever I've jumped into seemed to be halfway successful. It's just like a midsummer's night dream I guess—but I stuck with the dream. I've heard more about dreamin' since Martin Luther King's been on the scene and since he died. People have the dreams, and that's all. They never analyze the dream. Most of them don't know what the dream is and don't know what the dream means themselves, but we need more dreamers who will not only dream, but take the dream, tear it to pieces, analyze every part of it, and work it out for all it's worth. That's what King did. That's what I did—stick with it. I can't do it all by myself. Most of the guys are looking out for themslves and aren't looking out for anybody else. Even the schoolkids, even the guys at the universities. They ain't bothered about it—they just peform, you know.

TAYLOR. Where do you think gospel music is going from here?

DORSEY. Now that's a question I'm not bothered about. All I want is to stay in Chicago as long as I'm here. I think I'll be here for a long time.

Chronological List
Copyright Dates of
Thomas Andrew Dorsey's Music

R = Renewal

1920

1. "If You Don't Believe I'm Leaving Count the Days"
    (W&M) L. Smith and T. A. Dorsey

1921

No new titles copyrighted.

1922

1. "If I Don't Get There"

1923

1. "Blue Monday Blues"
    (W&M) Alva White and T. A. Dorsey
2. "Don't Shimmy No More"
    (W&M) T. A. Dorsey and Jone Meake

3. "Heart There Was for You"

4. "I Just Want a Daddy I Can Call My Own"

5. "Miss Anna Brown Blues"

6. "Riverside Blues"

7. "That Brown of Mine"

1924

1. "Blue Monday Blues" ®

     (W&M) Alva White

2. "Carolina Blues"

3. "Chicago Monkey Man Blues"

     (W) J. M. Williams, Ida Cox, and T. A. Dorsey

4. "Eagle Rock Me, Papa"

5. "Freight Train Blues"

     (W&M) Everett Murphy and T. A. Dorsey

6. "Last Minute Blues"

7. "When All the Saints Go Marching In"

8. "Wild Women Don't Have the Blues"

     (W&M) Althea Dickerson and T. A. Dorsey

1925

1. "Explaining the Blues"

2. "Memphis Bound Blues"

3. "Night Time Blues"

     (W&M) Ma Rainey and T. A. Dorsey

4. "Stormy Sea Blues"

1926

1. "Chain Gang Blues"
   (W) J. Parker
2. "Get Your Early Told"
3. "My Lord's Gonna Move This Wicked Race"
4. "Slave to the Blues"
5. "The Creole Band"
   (M&W) Albert Wynn T. A. Dorsey
6. "When"

1927

No new titles copyrighted.

1928

1. "Assembly-ville"
2. "Awful Lawdy Lawdy Blues"
3. "Black Cat Hoot Owl"
4. "Blame It on the Blues"
5. "Christmas Man Blues"
6. "Ethiopia Shall Remember You"
7. "Gonna Catch You with Your Breaches Down"
8. "Grieving Me Blues"
10. "It's Tight like That"
11. "Loafin' Blues"
12. "Long Ago Blues"

13. "Looking for the Blues"
14. "Love's Sweet Unity"
15. "My Beedle Um Bum"
16. "Rolling Mill"
17. "Rose-Buds"
18. "Selling That Stuff"
19. "Victim to the Blues"
20. "When You're in Love"

1929

1. "Don't Drink It Here"
2. "Hokum Boys from Tennessee"
3. "I Ain't Gonna Do It No More"
4. "I Had to Give Up My Gymnasium"
5. "It's So Nice"
6. "It's Tight like That"
7. "Lonesome Man Blues"
8. "Only the Blues"
9. "Parkway Stomp"
10. "Pat-a-foot Blues"
11. "Pat That Bread"
12. "Some Cold Rainy Day"
13. "That's the Way She Likes It"
14. "Then My Gal's in Town"
15. "Voice of the Blues"
16. "You Ain't Livin' Right"
17. "You Can't Cheat a Cheater"

1930

1. "Blue Moanin' Blues"
2. "Come on Mama Do That Dance for Me"
3. "Doctor's Blues"
4. "Eagle Ridin' Papa"
5. "Gee, But It's Hard"
6. "Hear Me Beefin' at You"
7. "Kunjine Baby"
8. "Maybe It's the Blues"
9. "Nancy Jane"
10. "Papa's Gettin' Hot"
11. "Pig Meat Blues"
12. "Six Shooter Blues"
13. "Terrible Operation"
14. "Tomorrow Blues"
15. "You Got Me in This Mess"
16. "You Got That Stuff"

1931-1934

No new titles copyrighted

1935

1. "Where Did You Stay Last Night?"

1936

1. "Caught Us Doing It"
2. "If You Sing a Gospel Song"
3. "I'm Talkin' 'bout Jesus"

1937

No new titles copyrighted.

1938

1. "Get Ready and Serve the Lord"
2. "I'm Gonna Walk Right In and Make Myself at Home"
3. "Hide Me in Thy Bosom"
4. "If Jesus Bore His Cross, So Can I"
5. "I'll Tell It Wherever I Go"
6. "I'm Gonna Hold on 'Til Jesus Comes"
7. "Make Me the Servant I Would Like to Be"
8. "My Desire"
9. "Something New Burning in My Soul"
10. "Take My Hand, Precious Lord"
11. "Who Is Willing to Take a Stand for the Lord?"

1939-1945

No new titles copyrighted.

1946

No new titles copyrighted.

1947

1. "Piano Duet, Book of Gospel Hymns"

1948

No new titles copyrighted.

1949

1. "He Is the Same Today"
2. "He Never Will Leave Me"
3. "He's All I Need"
4. "Hide Me in Thy Bosom" ®
5. "How Many Times"
6. "How Much More of Life's Burden Can We Bear?"
7. "I Don't Know Why I Have to Cry"
8. "Let Me Understand"
9. "Search Me Lord"
10. "Tell Jesus Everything"
11. "That's Good News"
12 "The Lord Will Make a Way Somehow"
13. "This Man, Jesus"
14. "Today" (Evening Song)
15. "What Could I Do If It Wasn't for the Lord?"

1950

1. "Be Thou Near Me All the Way: Prayer of the Righteous"
2. "Don't Forget the Name of the Lord"
3. "Everyday Will Be Sunday By and By"
4. "Give Me a Voice to Sing Thy Praise"
5. "God Be with You"
6. "He Is Risen"
7. "How About You?"
8. "I Am on the Battlefield for My Lord"
9. "I Can Depend on Jesus"
10. "I Claim Jesus First and That's Enough"
11. "If Jesus Bore His Cross, So Can I"
12. "If We Never Needed the Lord Before, We Sure Need Him Now"
13. "If You Meet God in the Morning"
14. "I'll Tell It Wherever I Go"
15. "I'm Going to Live the Life I Sing About in My Song"
16. "I'm Goin' to Wait Until My Change Shall Come"
17. "I'm Going to Walk Right In and Make Myself at Home"
18. "I'm Waiting for Jesus. He's Waiting for Me"
19. "I Want Jesus on the Road I Travel"
20. "Inside the Beautiful Gate"
21. "Jesus Only"
22. "Jesus Remembers When Others Forget"
23. "Jesus Rose Again"
24. "Just One Step"
25. "Just Wait a Little While"
26. "Old Ship of Zion"
27. "Remember Me" (We Shall Be Remembered by Our Works)

28. "Someday I'm Going to See My Savior"
29. "Somewhere"
30. "Take My Hand, Precious Lord"
31. "Thank You for All the Days of My Life"
32. "The Lord Has Laid His Hands on Me"
33. "The Lord Knows Just What I Need"
34. "The Savior Is Born"
35. "There'll Be Peace in the Valley for Me"
36. "There Is No Friend Like Jesus"
37. "There's a God Somewhere"
38. "Today" (Evening Song) *
39. "Traveling On"
40. "Walking Up the King's Highway"
41. "When I've Done My Best"
42. "When the Gates Swing Open, Let Me In"
43. "Your Sins Will Find You Out"

1951

1. "Come Unto Me"
2. "Does It Mean Anything to You?"
3. "God Is Good to Me"
4. "I Just Can't Keep from Crying Sometime"
5. "I Know My Redeemer Lives"
6. "I'm a Stranger"
7. "I May Never Pass This Way Again"
8. "I'm Going to Hold on 'Til Jesus Comes for Me"
9. "I'm Going to Work Until the Day Is Done"
10. "I Thank God for My Song"

11. "It's a Blessing Just to Call My Savior's Name"
12. "It's Not a Shame to Cry Holy to the Lord"
13. "I Want to Go There"
14. "I Will Trust in the Lord"
15. "Keep Praying All the Time"
16. "Lead Me to the Rock That's Higher Than I"
17. "Let Me Understand"
18. "Let Us Go Back to God"
19. "Life Can Be Beautiful"
20. "Look on the Brighter Side"
21. "Lord, Look Down Upon Me"
22. "Meet Me at the Pearly Gate"
23. "My Soul Feels Better Right Now"
24. "Never Leave Me Alone"
25. "Peace, It's Wonderful"
26. "Somebody's Knocking at Your Door"
27. "Someday I'm Coming Home"
28. "Someday, Somewhere"
29. "Someway, Somehow, Sometime, Somewhere"
30. "Take Me Through, Lord"
31. "The Little Wooden Church on the Hill"
32. "There Is Something about the Lord Mighty Sweet"
33. "There's an Empty Chair at the Table"
34. "The Savior's Here"
35. "Thy Kingdom Come"
36. "Use My Heart, Use My Mind, Use My Hands"
37. "Walk Close to Me, O Lord"
38. "Want to Go to Heaven When I Die"
39. "Watching and Waiting"

40. "What the Good Lord's Done for Me"
41. "When Day Is Done"
42. "When I've Sung My Last Song"
43. "When the Last Mile Is Finished"
44. "When They Crown Him Lord of All"

1952

1. "Count Your Blessings from the Lord Each Day"
2. "Forgive Me Lord and Try Me One More Time"
3. "I'm Climbing Up the Rough Side of the Mountain"
4. "Just Look Around"
5. "Never Leave Me Alone"
6. "Old Time Spirituals—Medley No. 1"
7. "Shake My Mother's Hand for Me"
8. "Someway, Somehow, Sometime, Somewhere" ®
9. "The Day Is Past and Gone"

1953

1. "Consideration"
2. "If You See My Savior"
3. "I'm Just a Sinner Saved by Grace"
4. "An Angel Spoke to Me Last Night"
5. "Diamonds from the Crown of the Lord"
6. "I'm Coming Back Home to Live with Jesus"
7. "It Is Thy Servant's Prayer Amen"
8. "Shake My Mother's Hand for Me" ®

1954

1. Angels Keep Watching Over Me
2. It Doesn't Cost Very Much
3. "My Faith I Place in Thee"
4. "Something Has Happened to Me"
5. "Walking Up the King's Highway" ®
6. "Walk Over God's Heaven"
7. "While the Evening Shadows Fall, There's Morning My Heart"

1955

1. "Let the Savior Bless Your Soul Right Now"
2. "Standing Here Wondering Which Way to Go"
3. "Windows of Heaven"

1956

1. "I Have a Home"
2. "I'm Getting More like Jesus Every Day"
3. "I'll Be Waiting for You at the Beautiful Gate"
4. "I Thought of God"
5. "Let Every Day Be Christmas"
6. "Look Up"
7. "Someday I'll Be at Rest"

1957

1. "Beautiful Tomorrow"
2. "Behold, the Man of Galilee"

3. "Every Day Will Be Sunday By and By" ®
4. "Maybe It's the Place"
5. "Say a Little Prayer for Me"
6. "There'll Be Peace in the Valley" ®
7. "You Got That Stuff"

1958

1. "Down by the Side of the River"
2. "Hold Me Please and Don't Let Me Go"
3. "I Can't Understand"
4. "In the Scheme of Things"
5. "It's a Highway to Heaven"

1959

1. "Army Rock"
2. "Blue Melody"
3. "Boots, Boots"
4. "Dorsey's Songs with a Message"
5. "Do You Know Anything about Jesus?"
6. "Gospel Melody"
7. "Go with Me"
8. "He Has Gone to Prepare a Place for Me"
9. "Hold On a Little While Longer"
10. "I Don't Know What I'd Do without the Lord"
11. "I Got Heaven in My View"
12. "I'll Take Jesus for Mine"
13. "I'm Satisfied with Jesus in My Heart"
14. "I'm Singing Every Day"

15. "In My Savior's Care"

16. "It Is Real with Me"

17. "It's All in the Plan of Salvation"

18. "I Want to Be More like Jesus"

19. "I Want Two Wings to Veil My Face"

20. "Let Us Pray Together"

21. "McClellan Theme"

22. "My Lord's Going to Move This Wicked Race"

23. "O Lord, Show Me the Way"

24. "Opening Theme"

25. "Shake My Mother's Hand for Me" ®

26. "She Is Mine"

27. "Singing in My Soul"

28. "Southern Melody"

29. "Surely My Jesus Must Be True"

30. "Sworn to Stick Together"

31. "Take My Hand, Precious Lord" ®

32. "Ta-ta-ta"

33. "Troubled about My Soul"

34. "War Theme"

35. "What's at Harper's Ferry?"

36. "Won't You Come and Go Along"

37. "You Can't Go Through This World by Yourself"

38. "You've Got to Righten Each Wrong Someday"

1960

1. "Do You Know Anything about Jesus?"

2. "He Has Gone to Prepare a Place for Me"

3. "I Don't Know What I'd Do without the Lord" ®

4. "I'm Satisfied with Jesus"

5. "I'm Singing Every Day"

6. "It Is Real with Me"

7. "My Lord's Going to Move This Wicked Place" *

8. "O Lord, Fix Me"

9. "O Lord, Show Me the Way"

10. "Troubled about My Soul"

1962

1. "Did You Ever Say to Yourself That I Love Jesus?"

2. "I Am on the Battlefield for My Lord"

3. "I Know Jesus"

4. "I'm Satisfied with Jesus in My Heart"

5. "I Thought on My Way"

6. "It's All in the Plan of Salvation"

7. "You've Got to Righten Each Wrong Someday" *

1963

1. "If I Walk with Him"

2. "If You Sing a Gospel Song"

3. "I'm Talking about Jesus"

4. "Jesus Never Does a Thing That's Wrong"

5. "Save Me as I Am"

6. "There's a Brighter Day Coming Right Here"

7. "Where Did You Stay Last Night?"

1964

1. "I'm Just a Sinner Saved by Grace"
2. "Jesus Lives in Me"
3. "My Desire"
4. "While He's Passing By"

1965

1. "Forgive My Sins, Forget, and Make Me Whole"
2. "Get Ready and Serve the Lord"
3. "Going to Walk Right In and Make Myself at Home"
4. "Go with Me"
5. "Hide Me in Thy Bosom"
6. "If Jesus Bore This Cross, So Can I" ®
7. "If You Don't Dig the Blues"
8. "I'll Tell It Wherever I Go"
9. "I'm Going to Hold On 'Til Jesus Comes for Me" ®
10. "Jesus Is the Light"
11. "Make Me the Servant I'd Like to Be" ®
12. "Maybe It's You and Maybe It's Me"
13. "Not Too Old to Cry"
14. "Something New Burning in My Soul" ®
15. "Who Is Willing to Take a Stand for My Lord?" ®

1966

1. "Great Gospel Songs"
2. "Hide Me in Thy Bosom" ®

3. "Hide Me, Jesus, in the Solid Rock"
4. "I'm Coming Back Home"
5. "It Is Thy Servants Prayer Amen"
6. "Keep Praying All the Time"
7. "Remember Me"
8. "The Little Town Where I First Saw the Lord"
9. "Today"
10. "When I've Done My Best"
11. "When the Last Mile Is Finished"
12. "Wings over Jordan"

1967

1. "All Is Well"
2. "Does It Mean Anything to You?"
3. "God Be with You"
4. "How Many Times?"
5. "If You Meet God in the Morning"
6. "I Know My Redeemer Lives"
7. "Just for You"
8. "Life Can Be Beautiful"
9. "My Time's Not as Long as It Has Been"
10. "Our Father, Who Art in Heaven"
11. "Singing My Way to Rest"
12. "Today"
13. "Walking Up the King's Highway"
14. "Wasn't That an Awful Time?"

1968

1. "He Is Risen for He's Living in My Soul"
2. "How Many Times?"
3. "I'm Going to Sing the Song I Sing about in My Song"
4. "Just Wait a Little While"
5. "Sometimes My Burden's So Hard to Bear"
6. "Somewhere" *
7. "There's an Empty Chair at the Table"
8. "Walk Close to Me, O Lord"

1969

1. "How about You?"
2. "I Can Depend on Jesus, He Can Depend on Me"
3. "I Claim Jesus First and That's Enough for Me"
4. "I Don't Know Why I Have to Cry Sometime"
5. "I Thank God for My Song"
6. "I Want Jesus on the Road I Travel"
7. "I Want to Go There"
8. "Jesus Never Does a Thing That's Wrong"
9. "Jesus Remembers When Others Forget"
10. "Let Us Go Back to God"
11. "Someday, Somewhere"
12. "Something Has Happened to Me"
13. "The Flag for You and Me"
14. "The Lord Knows Just What I Need"
15. "There's a God Somewhere"
16. "Use My Heart, Use My Mind, Use My Hands"
17. "What the World Needs Is Jesus Most of All"

18. "When the Gates Swing Open Let Me In"
19. "When You Bow in the Evening at the Altar"

1970

1. "Be There Near Me All the Way"
2. "God Is Good to Me"
3. "If We Ever Needed the Lord Before"
4. "Let Me Understand"
5. "Thy Kingdom Come"
6. "When I've Sung My Last Song"
7. "Yes"

1971

1. "He's All I Need"
2. "I'll Never Turn Back"
3. "I'm Going to Wait Until My Change Comes"
4. "Lord, Look Down on Me"
5. "Take Me Through, Lord"
6. "What Could I Do If It Wasn't for the Lord?"

1972

1. "Come On In"
2. "Hold On a Little While Longer"
3. "I Got Jesus in My Soul"
4. "I'm Waiting for Jesus, He's Waiting for Me"
5. "Somebody's Knocking at Your Door"
6. "That's All That I Can Do"

1973

1. "Come Unto Me" *
2. "There Isn't but One Way to Make It In"
3. "Your Sins Will Find You Out"

1974

1. "Every Day Will Be Sunday By and By" *
2. "I May Never Pass This Way Again"
3. "It's Not a Shame to Cry Holy to the Lord"
4. "Someday in Your Home"
5. "Somewhere Now"
6. "Thank You All the Days of My Life"
7. "When the Day Is Done"

Bibliography

Books

Bontemps, Arna Wendell and Langston Hughes, eds. *The Book of Negro Folklore*. New York: Dodd, Mead, 1958.

Heilbut, Tony, *The Gospel Found: Good News and Bad Times*. New York: Simon and Schuster, 1971.

Lovell, John, Jr., *Black Song*. New York: The Macmillan Company, 1972.

"Music Published by Thomas A. Dorsey," in the *Catalog of Copyright Entries: Third Series*. Washington: Copyright Office, the Library of Congress, 1947-1974.

Patterson, Lindsay, *Rock, Church, Rock*. New York: Publishers Company Inc., 1967-1969.

Southern, Eileen, *The Music of Black Americans: A History*. New York: W. W. Morton, 1971.

Periodicals

Heckman, Don. "Rhythm and Blues." *Broadcast Music Incorporated,* Summer Issue (1969): 23.

Tallmadge, William H. "The Responsorial and Antiphonal Practice in Gospel Songs." *Ethnomusicology* 12 (May 1968): 219.

Microfilm Reproductions

U.S Copyright Office, <u>Music New Series, Published Music by Thomas A. Dorsey</u>, 1920-1946.

Interview

Dorsey, Thomas Andrew, Chicago, Illinois, Interview, 1 January 1975.

ADDENDUM

T.A.D. Selected Published Songs

Title	Year
1. Did You Ever Say To Your-Self	1962
2. He Never Will Leave Me	1949
3. Standing Here Wondering	1955
4. There's A God Somewhere	1942
5. The Savior is Born	1950
6. You Can't Go Through This World	1933

DID YOU EVER SAY TO YOUR-SELF THAT I LOVE JESUS?

A STANDARD HYMN
BY
THOMAS A. DORSEY

FOR CHOIR-CHORUS OR SOLO

PRICE 25 CENTS

Published by
THOMAS A. DORSEY, MUSIC PUBLISHER,
4154 S. Ellis Avenue, Chicago 53, Illinois.

Did You Ever Say To Your-Self That I Love Jesus?

A DORSEY HYMN

Words and Music by
THOMAS A. DORSEY

Then you be-gan to won-der____ and said it can't be true You
Hus-band, the wife, the chil-dren____ no mat-ter what they do You

loved and loved with all you had, and you thought that they loved you. But
love and love with all you have, and you hope that they love you. But

Did you ev-er say to your-self that I love Je - sus,
Did you ev-er say to your-self that I love Je - sus,

Did you ev-er say to your-self that He loves me, ____ O
Did you ev-er say to your-self He died for me, ____ O

Did you ev-er say to your-self that I love Je - sus, O
Did you ev-er say to your-self that I love Je - sus, O

Did You Ever Say To Your-Self That I Love Jesus - 3

PILGRIM CHORUS

Did you ev - er say to your - self that He loves me._____
Did you ev - er say to your - self He set me free._____

He loves me_____ He loves me_____
Did you ev-er say to your-self that Did you ev-er say to your-

He loves me_____ He loves me_____
self that Did you ev-er say to your-self that He loves me_____

_____ O Did you ev-er say to your-self that I love Je - sus, O

Did you ev - er say to your-self that He loves me._____

HE NEVER WILL LEAVE ME

by

THOMAS A. DORSEY

for

CHOIR, CHORUS OR SOLO

Featured by National Gospel Soloist Bureau
Willie Mae Ford Smith, Supervisor

PRICE **NEW PRICE**
25¢

T.A.D.

Published by
THOMAS A. DORSEY
755 OAKWOOD BLVD., CHICAGO 15, ILL.

MADE IN U.S.A.

He Never Will Leave Me

Featured by National Gospel Soloist Bureau
Willie Mae Ford Smith Supervisor

A Dorsey Song

By THOMAS A. DORSEY

Moderato

He nev-er will leave me__ He's al-ways at my side Yes__ He'll nev-er__ de-ceive me__ no mat-ter what be tide O__ I may some-time__ feel a-lone But He's some-where near by_____ and with me__ O His pres-ence__ a-bide.

VERSE

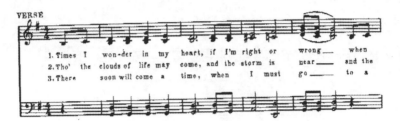

1. Times I won-der in my heart, if I'm right or wrong___ when
2. Tho' the clouds of life may come, and the storm is near___ and the
3. There soon will come a time, when I must go___ to a

trou-ble still ad - vanc-es af - flic - tions are pro-longed But faith holds me
rain may beat up - on me winds may en - hance my fear But I have His
place that's free from trou-ble and sor - rows are no more Where love one are

stead-y___ and cour - age___ makes me strong___ Then I
prom - ise___ when hope is___ al - most gone___ He is
wait - ing___ and man - y___ friends are gone___ Then He'll

re - al - ize I'm not left a - lone.___
with me and I'm not left a - lone.___ Now
nev - er nev - er leave me a - lone.___

He Never Will Leave Me-3

4

SPECIAL CHORUS

He nev-er___ will leave me___ He's al - ways at my

Yes He nev-er nev-er leave me Yes He's al-ways at my

side He'll nev-er___ de - ceive me___ no

al-ways at my side He will nev-er not de-ceive me

mat - ter what be - tide I may some-time feel a - lone But He's

no mat-ter what be-tide, well I may some-time some-time feel a-lone

some-where near by___ and with me___ His pres-ence a - bide.___

But He's some-where near by and with me His pres - ence a - bide.

He Never Will Leave Me-3

STANDING HERE WONDERING WHICH WAY TO GO

by

THOMAS A. DORSEY

FOR CHOIR, CHORUS OR SOLO

PRICE ~~35¢~~ New Price - 50¢   T.A.D.

PUBLISHED BY

THOMAS A. DORSEY, PUBLISHER

4154 So. Ellis Avenue, Chicago, Illinois. 60653

MADE IN U.S.A.

Standing Here Wondering Which Way To Go

A DORSEY SONG

Words and Music by
THOMAS A. DORSEY

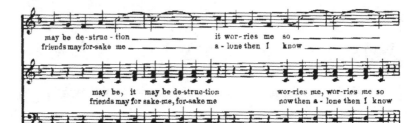

VERSE

1. The road lay in dark - ness _____ The lights burn-ing low _____ Now
2. My moth-er's in heav - en _____ My fa-ther must go _____ My

dark-ness, in dark-ness in dark-ness lights bur-ning, lights burning low
moth-er's in, moth-er's in heav-en fa-ther must, fa-ther must go

where will it lead us _____ no one seems to know _____ It
sis - ter must leave me _____ my broth-er's for sure _____ My

where will it, where will it lead us no one down here seems to know
sis - ter must sis - ter must leave me broth-er's my broth-er's for sure

may be de-struc - tion _____ it wor-ries me so _____
friends may for-sake me _____ a - lone then I know _____

may be, it may be de-struc-tion wor-ries me, wor-ries me so
friends may for sake-me, for-sake me now then a - lone then I know

Lord if you know me, come here and show me, which way to go. _____

know me, come here and show me, which way to go. which way to go.

4

I'm stand-ing here wond-'ring _____ which way to go _____

Hum   Hum Hum   Hum   Hum Hum

so much con-fu-sion _____ in this world be-low _____ I've

Hum   Hum Hum   Hum   Hum Hum

start-ed for Heav-en _____ to land on that shore _____ I'm

Hum   Hum Hum   Hum   Hum Hum

stand-ing here wond-'ring wond-'ring and won-der-ing which way we go _____

Hum   Hum   Hum   Hum   Hum Hum _____

D.C. al Fine

Standing Here Wondering etc.-8

Dedicated to the W. Va. State Singing Convention, A. J. Jones Pres

There's A God Some-Where

A Dorsey Song

THOMAS A. DORSEY

Organize a Gospel Chorus and use Dorsey's songs

The Savior is Born

Sung by 100 voice Gospel Chorus Pilgrim Bapt. Church, Chicago, Ill.

Thomas A. Dorsey, Dir.

A Dorsey Song

By THOMAS A. DORSEY
Writer of How About You

With Spirit

Well the Sav-ior is born Well the Sav-ior is born Well the Sav-ior is born They

found Him in a man-ger in Beth-le-hem Well the Sav-ior is born Well the Sav-ior is born

Well the Sav-ior is born They found Him in a man-ger in Beth-le-hem

1. The wise men came from far and near
2. The an-gels they be-gan to sing
3. The shep-herds watch'd their flock by night
4. They look'd for him four thou-sant years

Fine

Found Him in a man-ger in Beth-le-hem

They brought Him gifts good will and cheer
Peace on earth good will to men
When the star came in-to sight
To take a-way all doubt and fears

Found Him in a man-ger in Beth-le-hem.

Songs that carry a message!

Watching and Waiting 10c
Precious Lord   10c

What Then   10c
Traveling On 10c

Shaking My Mother's Hand 10c
My Mind On Jesus   10c

Do not print ballads of these songs —— Penalty

You Can't Go Through This World By Yourself.

A Dorsey Song
Songs that carry a message

As sung by Miss Josie Fisher and Gospel Chorus, Cairo, Ill.

Poem by
THOMAS A. DORSEY
Writer of "Inside That Beautiful Gate"

Photos and Memorial Services contributed

by Dr. Lena McLin, Mr. Dorsey's Niece

Past Times Photo Mr. Dorsey and Singer

Mr. Dorsey

Memorial Services Year 1993

Memorial Services

Celebrating The Life

Of

THOMAS A. DORSEY

1899 - 1993

7:00 P.M.

Saturday, January 30, 1993

Greater Mount Calvary Baptist Church
388 Glenn Street, S.W.
Atlanta, Georgia

Reverend B. J. Johnson, Jr.
Pastor

BIOGRAPHICAL SKETCH

*Next to God and theology there was a man, **Thomas A. Dorsey**, who chose a virgin sheet, dipped his pen in the blood of life, and through thought, verses, and rhythmic sounds "Gospel music" became a reality.*

B.J.J., Jr.

Thomas Andrew Dorsey, son of Reverend Thomas Madison and Etta Dorsey, was born July 1, 1899 in Villa Rica, Georgia thirty miles west of Atlanta, Georgia. When he was a young boy, his musical talent, which was nurtured by his mother, was evident. He reported that he could play piano "very well" at age twelve. He started his music career by playing at saloons, special parties, dancehalls and theaters. He earned the name "Barrelhouse Tom and "Georgia Tom" from playing lively music and joined Ma Rainey's Band on the road as her musical director. Dorsey also attended Morehouse College

Dorsey moved to Chicago in 1916, he worked in the steel mills and attended the Chicago Musical College. In the early 1920's he coined the term "Gospel Songs." After listening to songs of a group of five people at a southside Chicago church. Still helping the jazz musicians, Thomas played for the South Side Baptist Church. It was 1921 at the National Baptist Convention where Thomas heard religious singing and wanted to do music to accompany it.

While ill in 1926, Thomas wrote "Somewhere, Someday" and "If You See My Savior." He sent out 500 songs with $5.00 worth of one cent stamps. Almost giving up on Gospel music because of no response, it was three years later before he received his first order for Gospel music - something that was not accepted in his day because of its bluesy elements.

Thomas used to go town-to-town selling his music for ten cents a copy. In 1929, he published the first gospel song, "If You See My Savior." He heard the term "Singing To The Gospel," thus the words gospel music developed. He was the first publisher of Gospel Music as he opened his own publishing company that same year.

Thomas Dorsey and Theodore Frye formed the first gospel choir at Ebenezer Baptist Church in Chicago during 1930-31. He formed the first Gospel Chorus at Pilgrim Baptist Church. He, Frye and Magnolia Lewis Butts started the National Convention of Gospel Choirs, Inc. in 1932.

On the way to St. Louis, August 1932, Dorsey found out that his expectant wife Nettie died. That moved Dorsey to write the most famous Gospel Tune of all time...... sung in 80 countries, recorded by over 500 artists, "Precious Lord, Take My Hand." His healthy son also died the next day. Dorsey has since sung/directed this song in Paris, London, Rome, Athens, Cairo, Damascus, Beirut, Jerusalem and the West Indies. Other songs to follow were, "I've Got Heaven In My View," "Peace In The Valley," and over 2,000 songs-gospel and secular have been written and performed by Dorsey.

Dorsey was the first African American to be awarded the Nashville Songwriters Association International Hall of Fame Award in 1979. Dorsey received a Grammy Award for Life Time Achievement in 1992. Dorsey received the 1985 Illinois Governor's Award for the Arts, Songwriters Hall of Fame in New York (1982), Georgia Music Hall of Fame (1981), Gospel Music Association Living Hall of Fame (1982), and Doctor of Humane Letters from Fisk University, Selma and Howard University (1982). Served over 30 years as President of the National Convention of Gospel Choirs.

"Say Amen", a documentary about Dorsey and Gospel Music was nominated for an academy award for Best Documentary. His music has been performed by Mahalia Jackson and many, many others.

Dorsey was inducted in the National Hall of Fame. The Thomas A. Dorsey Music Festival in Chicago (which later became the Chicago Gospel Music Festival) is the largest worldwide gospel celebration to date.

He expired on Saturday, January 23, 1993 in Chicago, Illinois at the age of 93 years old.

ORDER OF SERVICE

Inez Mayfield, Presiding

Prelude

Processional

Organ and Piano Meditation

Hymn..................................*"O God Our Help In Ages Past"*...*Congregation*

Lesson from Old Testament................................*Psalm 23*.......................................*Reverend B. B. Carter*
                                                                                              Pastor, Union Baptist Church

Lesson from New Testament..................*I Corinthians 15:50-58*..................................*Reverend C. J. Maddox*
                                                                                    Pastor, Saint James First Baptist Church

Prayer...*Reverend   A. J. McMichael*
                                                                                       Pastor, Mount Nebo Baptist Church

Selection...*Greater   Mount Calvary Choir*

Remarks:

Governor's Office	*Honorable Carolyn Long Banks, City Council*
County Commissioners	*Honorable Rob Pitts, City Council*
Mayor's Office	*Honorable Bill Campbell, City Council*
Atlanta Police Department	

Selection...*Greater   Mount Calvary Choir*

Remarks:

Mr. Paul Martin *Georgia Music Workshop of America*	*Dr. Cornelius Henderson* *Pastor, Ben Hill United Methodist Church*
Ms. Eleanor Guest *Georgia Music Workshop of Amercia*	*Dr. C.M. Alexander* *Pastor, Antioch North Baptist Church* *President, General Missionary Baptist* *Convention of Georgia*
Mrs. Rosa Gresham *Greater Mount Calvary Baptist Church*	*Dr. Joseph Lowery* *President, SCLC*

Expressions In Songs:

Tabernacle Baptist Church *Sue Hampton Concert Choir*	*Mozell Patterson* *Inez Mayfield and Singers*
Georgia Music Workshop of America *Veronica Blakeney*	*Kenneth Lowe* *Jarvis Wilson* *Allwyn Crawford*
Morris Ector *Constance Small*	*Nellie Dorsey* *Gary Maddox*
and others to celebrate the Dorsey Gospel Memory	

Precious Lord...*Congregation*

Benediction..*Reverend   Mack Simons*
                                                                                        Pastor, Welcome All Baptist Church

Take My Hand, Precious Lord

Precious Lord, take my hand
Lead me on let me stand
I am tired, I am weak, I am worn

Thru the storm, thru the night
Lead me on to the light
Take my hand, Precious Lord
And lead me home.

When my way grows drear,
Precious Lord linger near
When my life is almost gone,
hear my cry, hear my call
Hold my hand, lest I fall,
Take my hand precious Lord and lead me home.

When the darkness appears,
And the night draws near
And the day is past and gone,
At the river I stand
Guide my feet hold my hand.
Take my hand, precious lord and lead me home.

Acknowledgement

The Dorsey family expresses thanks to all
and may God continue to bless you.

ACKNOWLEDGEMENTS

Special Thanks To:

Dr. Lena McLin
Dr. Eph Ehly
Rev. Charles P. Lucas
Mr. Calvin Morris
Ms. Serena Barnett